WITHDRAWN

CAREER PROFILES™

JOHN McCAIN

Profile of a Leading Republican

Kira Wizner

ROSEN
PUBLISHING®

New York

RODMAN PUBLIC LIBRARY

For my cousin, Pvt. Max "Mickey" Michiel. Died POW in Korea, April 22, 1951.

Published in 2008 by The Rosen Publishing Group, Inc.
29 East 21st Street, New York, NY 10010

Copyright © 2008 by The Rosen Publishing Group, Inc.

First Edition

All rights reserved. No part of this book may be reproduced in any form without permission in writing from the publisher, except by a reviewer.

Library of Congress Cataloging-in-Publication Data

Wizner, Kira.
John McCain : profile of a leading Republican / Kira Wizner. — 1st ed.
    p. cm. — (Career profiles)
Includes bibliographical references.
ISBN-13: 978-1-4042-1911-3
ISBN-10: 1-4042-1911-0
1. McCain, John, 1936—Juvenile literature. 2. Legislators—United States—Biography—Juvenile literature. 3. United States. Congress. Senate—Biography—Juvenile literature. 4. Prisoners of war—Vietnam—Biography—Juvenile literature. 5. Prisoners of war—United States—Biography—Juvenile literature. 6. United States Naval Academy—Biography—Juvenile literature. I. Title.
E840.8.M26W595 2007
328.73092—dc22
[B]

2006038329

Manufactured in Malaysia

38212005258014
Main Child Biography
MCCAIN   jB
M121w   OCT - - 2008
Wizner, Kira
John McCain : profile of a
leading Republican

CONTENTS

INTRODUCTION

Today, John McCain is one of the leading political figures in the United States. He is a tremendously influential and respected senator who many people believe will be our next president. It has been a remarkable rise for a boy who was nicknamed McNasty in high school, who graduated near the bottom of his class in college, and who was embroiled in one of the more infamous political scandals of our era. But if you examine McCain's life closely, you see that many of the traits that caused him trouble also set him apart from the crowd: confidence, courage, and independence in his thinking. In addition,

A confident John McCain strides to the podium at the 2000 Republican National Convention in Philadelphia. During his speech, he spoke about the importance of U.S. military strength.

McCain's brashness, his quick temper, and his defiance of authority all are qualities that enabled him to pursue political leadership.

Born into a military family in which both his father and grandfather were high-ranking navy officers, McCain learned early on that there was no higher calling than serving one's country. Of his father and grandfather, McCain wrote in his book *Faith of My Fathers*, "They were my first heroes . . . earning their respect has been the most lasting ambition of my life." Following in their footsteps, McCain charted a course to become a navy officer and eventually found himself flying combat missions in Vietnam.

Things did not go well. Shot down and captured by the North Vietnamese, McCain became a prisoner of war (POW), enduring years of torture and solitary confinement. He survived this grueling ordeal and came home to America a stronger person with clearer goals. He stayed in the navy but began to feel that he could do more for his country as a politician. When he ran for Congress and won, many people seemed surprised, but McCain never doubted himself.

When McCain came back from Vietnam, his hair had turned white prematurely as a result of malnutrition and poor treatment during his time in the

POW camp. This, along with his reputation as a boundlessly energetic worker, earned him the nickname the "White Tornado."

As an officer, a prisoner of war, a U.S. congressman and senator, McCain has served. In 2000, he ran for the nomination to serve his country in the ultimate capacity, as president, and he will run again in 2008. His inner strength has helped him through horrifying imprisonment and political scandal, and he has emerged as one of the country's leading Republicans. This is John McCain's story.

A Childhood on the Move

On August 29, 1936, John Sidney McCain III was born at the Coco Solo Naval Air Base hospital in the Panama Canal Zone, Panama. The Canal Zone was an important strategic asset protected by a fleet of U.S. warships. The baby's father, John McCain II, was a submarine commander stationed close by. His grandfather, John McCain Senior, a naval aviator known as "Slew" McCain, was in charge of the Coco Solo base at the time.

The McCains: A Navy Family

John McCain II, known as Jack, was a navy father. His children, like most

Infant John McCain is held by grandfather Admiral John "Slew" McCain in this family portrait. McCain's sister Alexandra, father Jack McCain, and mother Roberta Wright McCain round out the clan.

CAREER PROFILES

McCAIN

children of military personnel, never lived in one place for too long. Shortly after his son John was born, Jack was transferred to New London, Connecticut. This would be the first of many moves. Young John McCain showed signs of being a challenger from the beginning. By age two he was having temper tantrums and holding his breath until he passed out. McCain's navy doctor advised his parents to put him fully clothed into a tub of cold water! This shocking treatment ended the breath-holding spells but did not squelch his quick temper, a trait that the media and fellow politicians have commented on over the years.

The navy's unpredictable schedule and lifestyle were hard on the entire McCain family, and each member dealt with it in different ways. Father Jack worked increasingly longer hours. Mother Roberta Wright McCain focused more and more on managing the family and the budget. Although she came from a wealthy family, she wasn't frequently extravagant. But one time when she left the house to buy a dress, she came home with a Mercedes instead.

An Ever-Changing Life

Depending upon the assignment, both McCain's father and grandfather could be gone for days, weeks, or even months. They traveled a lot, but their presence was still felt in the McCain household. McCain's mother was very fond of her father-in-law. In their *Time* magazine article titled "Fathers, Sons and Ghosts," authors Michael Duffy and Nancy Gibbs wrote that Roberta McCain "would wake up the kids [McCain, his older sister

McCain's grandfather, Admiral John "Slew" McCain *(left)*, exchanges greetings with Major General Alexander Vandergrift (commander of marines battling at Guadalcanal), at the Solomon Islands, 1942.

Alexandra, and his younger brother Joseph] in the middle of the night and sit them on the sofa so she could take pictures of them with their famous grandfather."

McCain's mother was charged with moving the family every few years. Driving across the country, she had to listen to her children bicker and complain, but she made sure that these trips had a second purpose. About his mother, McCain wrote in his book *Character Is Destiny*, "She took us to dozens of famous art galleries, museums, and historical sites. Our jaws dropped in awe at the Grand Canyon, the Carlsbad Caverns."

McCain ascribes much of his personality to his mother. He wrote in his book *Faith of My Fathers*, "It is no surprise that the personalities of children who have grown up in the Navy often resemble those of their mothers more than their fathers." Some of the qualities of his mother's personality are exaggerated in McCain's own personality— while she is energetic and charming, he can work like a whirlwind and be a bit loud. McCain inherited her enthusiasm for life and formed a bond with his mother that has been life-long. When Pearl Harbor was bombed in December 1941, McCain's father left the house at once for his office, shipping off for a year a few months later. McCain has said of that time, "I became my mother's son."

Even before Pearl Harbor, McCain's father was, like some military dads, a military man first. For example, even on Christmas, his father would head out to the office. When McCain was young, his father's unavailability was hard for him to understand. It seemed to the young McCain that work always came first, even before family. Jack McCain was a larger-than-life figure, one that his son seems to have done battle with over the years. As an adult, McCain

The McCain males—young John (center) with, left to right, younger brother Joseph, his grandfather, and his father.

revisited that assessment, and wrote in *Faith of My Fathers*, "I am certain that he wanted to share with me the warm affection that he and his father had shared. But he wanted me to know also that a man's life should be big enough to encompass both duty to family and duty to country. That can be a hard lesson for a boy to learn. It was a hard lesson for me."

During World War II, when McCain hardly saw his father or grandfather, they made a special visit to come speak to McCain's class—duty to the country was first, but they made time for young John. That visit stood out in his memory. The sacrifice a navy man makes for his country was one that McCain grew up with and greatly respects.

Growing Up

When John was nine years old, four days after World War II ended, his famous grandfather died. The boy spent the next summer with his paternal grandmother and his aunt in Coronado, California. There were expectations in the house: tea was served at four, dinner was at seven, and John would eat alone if he didn't arrive on time. He spent days exploring his father's book collection, reading such authors as Robert Louis Stevenson, Mark Twain, James Fennimore Cooper, and Booth Tarkington.

He devoured traditional adventure stories with plots that stressed right and wrong. McCain wrote in *Faith of My Fathers* that he not only attributes his lifelong love of reading to this experience, but also "the virtue of treating people fairly."

By the time John was twelve, the family was living in Washington, D.C. He attended St. Stephen's School, where he once again started showing a defiant side. His mother didn't see it until later, when she was driving the family over the summer to the children's grandmother, in Coronado. The first night of the trip she wrote a letter to her husband that John reprinted in *Faith of My Fathers*. "Guess what?" the note reads, "Guess who was a nuisance today? Johnny." She was surprised until, eventually, she realized that it wasn't just one day. From that time on, she later said, he "was a pain in the neck." McCain certainly lived up to the derisive name "military brat" given to the children of military personnel.

McCain blames his early troubles on the constant cycle of moving, attending a new school, making new friends, and moving again. He wasn't physically imposing, but he used his ability to fight (win or lose, it didn't matter) to establish himself in new environments. In the summer of 1949, with the war over, the family started moving around again while

John's father commanded various submarines. Finally, when Jack McCain was transferred over the summer to the West Coast, he and his wife realized the burden they were placing on their children with the endless adjustments. They made the decision to send all three of them to boarding schools that fall. Once again, McCain would be the "new kid."

T W O REBEL YELL

In the fall of 1951, John McCain started his sophomore year at Episcopal High School, an all-boys boarding school in Alexandria, Virginia. Many prominent southern families sent their sons there, but it was by no means a fancy boarding school. The living conditions were simple, with the rooms being curtained alcoves. By this time, McCain was a feisty teenager.

Fitting In and Falling Out

John did not have a great time in high school. He had his first of two experiences with hazing at Episcopal. All first-year students were called "rats," and it didn't take long until John was given the name "Worst Rat." He got into fights, and he scorned the dress code by wearing his required coat, shirt, and tie with dirty jeans and shoes he repaired with tape. The hazing consisted of earning demerits for infractions and receiving punishments from upperclassmen. John was never apologetic or self-effacing. The older students thought he had no reason to seem so arrogant: He was short, not particularly brilliant, and didn't come from the South like most of the other students. He earned some other nicknames that reflected his disdain for the culture at school—"Punk" and "Nasty," or sometimes, "McNasty." He was proud of his defiance and wore his nicknames like badges of honor. Such traits would serve him well later in his military career.

John McCain speaks lovingly about only one person from all of high school: William Bee Ravenel III, one of his English teachers and his junior varsity football coach. John knew that Ravenel could recognize something in him that other teachers could not, and he found it inspiring. John appreciated Ravenel's English class as well as the way Ravenel energized his players on the football field. His memories of Ravenel never paled.

During his senior year at Episcopal, John found himself presented with an opportunity to show his leadership skills and his ability to speak out. At the beginning of the year, the boys on the junior varsity football team had signed a pledge to uphold certain team standards. When one of the team members violated the pledge, it meant that he should be expelled from school. This particular member, however, hadn't actually signed the pledge. Moreover, he admitted his mistake before anybody discovered it,

Hazing

The term "hazing" refers to the behaviors requested of people when they join a social group or organization. As initiation into that group, hazing is usually seen as a time-honored tradition. Typically, an entire group is subjected to humiliating and degrading behaviors. With "subtle" hazing, there is generally nothing physically dangerous. Most subtle hazing involves such behaviors as demerits, depriving people of privileges, making someone a social outcast, or requiring people to use official titles while the hazees themselves are called by insulting nicknames. Harassment hazing is harsher and more demeaning than subtle hazing. Violent hazing, on the other hand, can often descend into criminal behavior. It may involve forcing people to do something illegal (for example, stealing) or dangerous (like drinking excessive amounts of alcohol). In the United States, between 1970 and 2005, at least sixty-one people died as a result of violent hazing.

and he clearly felt remorse. The coach, John's mentor Mr. Ravenel, was in charge of the team's discussion to decide the boy's fate. Most of the boys on the team were ready to kick the offender off the team, but John felt very strongly otherwise. He thought that since the teammate had not signed the pledge and had admitted his misdeed of his own accord, a fair decision would be to keep him on the team. John convinced his teammates, helped a bit by Mr. Ravenel's approval, and that was the end of the discussion. This understanding of "fair and just" would resurface often in McCain's life.

Going Away to College

As McCain approached high school graduation, his military destiny was about to begin. From an early age, McCain knew where he would be attending college. He remembers listening to his parents remark, "He's going to the Naval Academy," as if it were an unavoidable fact. Even though his grades were poor at Episcopal, McCain did brilliantly on his entrance examination for the academy. So, at the beginning of the summer in 1954, just after high school graduation, McCain's father drove his son to the United States Naval Academy in Annapolis, Maryland, just as his father had driven him years before.

Rules, regulations, and order hold sway at the U.S. Naval Academy in Annapolis, Maryland. In this photo from the 1940s, students march in lockstep during a ceremony.

It was a good summer. Freshmen, otherwise known as plebes, had the run of the campus. McCain became an undefeated boxer, despite having no previous boxing training. And he played by the rules. He found the summer relaxing, despite the hard work. Everything was new, even the vocabulary. For example, stairs were now called ladders; bathrooms were called heads. Above all, in this new order, honor was the most important. But you had to get through hazing first.

Thus began McCain's second hazing experience. September 1954 brought with it the return of the second-, third-, and fourth-year students, and they made sure the plebes all went through the same treatment that had been inflicted on them when they were freshmen. The hazing consisted of insults, a constant barrage of requests for information, and questions that demanded immediate answers. The purpose, at least in part, was to see who had the toughness to make it through. (Eventually, 25 percent of the class would drop out.)

Academically, McCain didn't do so well. He liked his history and English classes but disliked math and engineering. Fortunately for McCain, neither his grandfather nor his father had a brilliant school record for him to live up to. Still, McCain the plebe was constantly called out for lateness and sloppiness, and always with his last name included in the jibes. He constantly had to deal with others' perception that he was at Annapolis because of his father and grandfather, not on his own merit.

After the first year, things changed. McCain became the de facto leader of a group called the Bad Bunch. They would sneak off campus to drink and hang out with girls. At this point, McCain didn't have a problem getting a date. Being a bit of a rebel, he had a kind of sex appeal his male friends appreciated but didn't exactly understand. During his free time, McCain led his friends on mini-expeditions that were a lot of fun, though not always sanctioned.

Honor Among Us

McCain's commitment to honor stands out in an anecdote recounted by author Robert Timberg in his book *John McCain: An American Odyssey*. During his sophomore year, McCain and his class-mates were only one step above the lowly plebes. In the cafeteria one day, a senior—otherwise known as a firstie or a first-classman—started to berate a Filipino steward who was serving the senior's table. This went against procedure. Firsties could insult and abuse plebes, as custom had established, but not an employee. McCain was the only one in the entire cafeteria who did something about it. "Hey, mister," he finally called, "why don't you pick on someone your own size?" The firstie asked, "What did you say?" and McCain followed through, "I don't think it's fair for you to pick on that steward . . . he's doing the best he can. You're picking on him. That's what I said." In a rare turn of events, the angry firstie saw the serious look in McCain's eye and walked out of the cafeteria. McCain had his beliefs, and his strong sense of right and wrong gave him the courage to speak up.

JOHN SIDNEY McCAIN, III
Washington, D. C.
    John, better known as Navy's John Wayne, was always reputed to be one of our most colorful characters. Following his family forbears to our sacred shores, he thought the Navy way was the only way. A sturdy conversationalist and party man, John's quick wit and clever sarcasm made him a welcome man at any gathering. His bouts with the Academic and Executive Departments contributed much to the stockpile of legends within the hall. His prowess as an athlete was almost above reproach; that is, if he could resist the temptations offered by the blue dragon. John looks forward to a long and successful career in the Navy; he is a natural and will not need the luck we wish him.

Midshipman John McCain in his freshman photo from Annapolis, with the original caption above

McCain's confidence served him well during his later naval training. In 1957, McCain went on a training voyage on the destroyer USS *Hunt* in Rio de Janeiro, Brazil. During the training, he had great success learning to steer the ship. Somewhat similar to William Ravenel at Episcopal, Lieutenant Commander Eugene Ferrell took McCain under his wing. Ferrell, who had trained under Jack McCain (though McCain didn't know it then), would give McCain the controls, or the "conn," until McCain would mess up. At that point Ferrell would swear at him, McCain would start

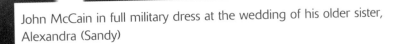

John McCain in full military dress at the wedding of his older sister, Alexandra (Sandy)

to leave the bridge, and Ferrell would call him back and teach him the right way. This pattern continued for the trip and McCain learned to steer the ship fairly well. Because of his early success, he was the only midshipman allowed to do this.

One afternoon, McCain had the conn when the *Hunt* needed to replenish its supplies from another ship. McCain, under Ferrell's watch, gave all the orders to steer the destroyer into place, and the entire maneuver went smoothly. While the boat was refueling, Ferrell sent a message to the admiral of the flagship: "Midshipman McCain has the conn." The admiral, impressed, passed on the information to the superintendent of the Naval Academy. It was a rare moment of positive recognition for McCain at Annapolis. Midshipmen were graded on their performance and, for his efforts, McCain received high marks.

The confidence and success gave McCain a burst of energy, leading him to work even harder as he began his final year at Annapolis. His grades improved, he started a tutoring program for plebes,

Joyful midshipmen and midshipwomen celebrate graduation day at Annapolis with the traditional hat toss. The U.S. Naval Academy is no longer an all-male institution, as it was when McCain attended.

McCAIN

and he managed the boxing team. Unfortunately, his other superiors weren't as helpful as Ferrell, and when McCain was told to keep up the good work, he was also reminded that his place was still at the bottom of the class. The McCain defiance reawakened, and he returned to the rebellious ways of his first three years. In the end, he graduated fifth from the bottom in his class, not so different from his father and grand-father. However, unlike his father and his grandfather, this McCain would be faced with horrors of war the elder two could hardly imagine.

THREE

SURVIVING VIETNAM

After Annapolis, McCain followed in his grandfather's footsteps and became a navy pilot, training on the naval air base in Pensacola, Florida. After he settled in, McCain once again set to spending more time on extracurricular social activities than he did on studying. Yet he still did well with the tasks he was given, and he was sent for advanced training in Corpus Christi, Texas. There, McCain had his first aircraft accident: His engine failed, and his plane went down in the water, sinking to the bottom. Luckily, he managed to get out and swim to the surface. McCain had his second major aircraft accident that December, when

C
A
R
E
E
R

P
R
O
F
I
L
E
S

an engine "flamed out" and he had to eject himself. Again, he escaped injury.

Navy Flier

McCain continued flying as a carrier pilot on the USS *Intrepid* and the USS *Enterprise*. Then, in 1964, he was sent back to Pensacola, working in the office, not training or flying. This was unsettling for McCain, who wanted to be flying combat missions as he had been trained to do. The Vietnam War was heating up, and like his father and grandfather before him,

Lieutenant John McCain *(standing, right)* poses with pilots from his squadron. At the time, McCain was a flight instructor, training pilots in basic jet aviation skills.

he wanted to be part of history. Asking to be put back on the active duty roster, he was assigned to be a flight instructor at McCain Air Base (named for his grandfather) in Meridian, Mississippi.

While he waited to be sent to war, McCain was working on a serious relationship with Carol Shepp, a model from Philadelphia whom he had known at Annapolis. Shepp was divorced from one of McCain's former classmates. She and McCain were married on July 3, 1965, in a small ceremony, and the following year, McCain adopted her two sons—Doug, who was

The Vietnam War

Begun in 1960, the Vietnam War, also called the Vietnam Conflict, was a battle between North Vietnam, which was Communist, and South Vietnam, which was anti-Communist. North Vietnam was allied with the Soviet Union and the People's Republic of China. South Vietnam was allied with the United States, Australia, and Thailand, among other countries.

The United States had been assisting the South Vietnamese military since 1950, but American troops were not deployed until 1965. The war ended in April 1975, when South Vietnam surrendered. The death toll for Vietnamese people is estimated between 1.5 and 3 million. For U.S. soldiers, the death toll was approximately 58,000. Vietnam is still under Communist rule today.

McCain *(far right)* and fellow pilots inspect damage on the deck of the USS *Forrestal*. The hole was made by the bomb that fell off McCain's plane as it was readied for a mission.

five, and Andy, who was three. In September 1966, Carol gave birth to their first child together, a daughter named Sydney.

The following spring, McCain was stationed to the USS *Forrestal*, soon to be heading to Vietnam. With three children under his roof, McCain would face the same challenges experienced by his own father, struggling to balance fatherhood with work and service to his country.

The USS *Forrestal* arrived at its station on July 25, 1966. Combat missions started immediately, and although he didn't know it, McCain was about to survive his third major aircraft incident. On July 29, as he was sitting in his cockpit ready to fly a mission, a huge explosion rocked the ship. An F-4 fighter plane on deck had accidentally fired a Zuni rocket straight into a 400-gallon fuel tank. The explo-

CAREER PROFILES

sion was massive, hundreds of seamen were injured, and 134 lost their lives. Bombs being stored underneath McCain's plane detonated, but McCain escaped from his aircraft and suffered only minor wounds, as small pieces of metal pierced his chest and legs.

Lieutenant Commander John McCain was then posted to the USS *Oriskany*. His mission was to fly and hit targets over Hanoi, the capital of North Vietnam. On his twenty-third mission, which was targeting a power plant in central Hanoi, his plane was hit by a surface-to-air missile. His radio message was, simply, "I'm hit." He ejected himself from the plane, falling into a lake in central Hanoi. The weight of McCain's equipment pulled him beneath the surface, but eventually he was able to pull a toggle button on his uniform, which released and inflated a life preserver. This aircraft incident would not end as fortunately as the others.

Taken Captive in Vietnam

Some North Vietnamese soldiers and a group of North Vietnamese civilians went into the lake and captured McCain, who had broken his arms and one of his legs. Showing little mercy—he was, after all, trying to bomb them—the crowd reportedly

Shot down above Hanoi, McCain ejected and landed in Truc Back Lake, where he was fished out—and beaten—by these North Vietnamese civilians.

bayoneted him in the foot and groin, and crushed his shoulder with the butt of a rifle. After being beaten, he was posed for propaganda photographs— a woman held a cup of tea as if she were helping him drink. Then they put the injured McCain in the back of a truck and drove him to the Hoa Lo prison, ironically called the Hanoi Hilton by American soldiers, as it was actually the complete opposite of a luxury facility.

His injuries were bandaged, but McCain was denied further medical treatment until he "talked." Giving just his name, rank, and serial number, in accordance with POW guidelines, he was beaten and left alone in a cell. McCain realized that his wounds were life-threatening and without medical attention, he would probably die. He tried to bargain with his captors—if they would bring him to a hospital, he would give them information after he was treated. They refused.

Later in the day, the North Vietnamese came to understand that McCain was the son of an admiral, which made this prisoner a special case. If he accepted offers to go home, McCain would be seen as soft, and he would embarrass the family and the government. But if McCain was killed or disfigured in captivity, the U.S. government might be spurred to retaliate. A North Vietnamese military official, whom McCain and his fellow prisoners renamed "the Bug," came to tell McCain he would be taken to the hospital. It was a horrible place, with roaches and rats, but at least he got sufficient treatment to avoid death.

Thus began a long and sometimes brutal hospital stay. McCain's arms wouldn't heal, even though North Vietnamese doctors tried to reset the bone (albeit without anesthesia, so the pain was excruciating). They didn't bathe or shave him, and he didn't have people to talk with. They prettied him up one day for an interview with a French journalist, François Chalais,

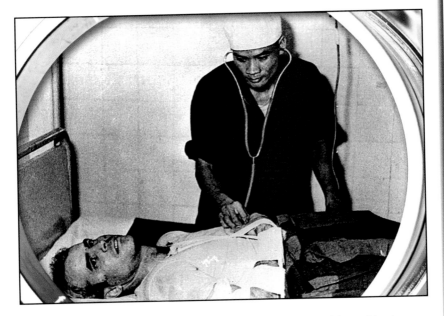

In this photo, taken mostly for show, McCain is treated by a North Vietnamese doctor. In reality, McCain's medical care throughout his captivity was woefully inadequate.

but McCain refused to say anything more than he had said already. He was determined to be like any other prisoner of war. He thought it would be dishonorable to receive any special treatment, and that would have been far worse for McCain's ego than anything else.

When McCain found out his arm wasn't healing well, his spirit declined, and he asked to be back with Americans. The next night, he was blindfolded and taken by truck to another prison, called the Plantation.

The Difficult Life of a Prisoner of War

At the Plantation, McCain was saved by fellow American solders. He was put in a cell with Bud Day and Norris Overly. Overly took McCain under his wing, spending days washing the encrusted dirt off McCain's face so he could eventually shave him. Overly also washed an injury to McCain's knee, which was becoming infected, and helped McCain go to the bathroom in the metal bucket provided. He also fed him.

Overly soon accepted a release offer, earning epithets as a "fink" for breaking ranks with his fellow captives. McCain, too, was offered release, but he vehemently refused. McCain didn't want any special treatment because of his lineage. He was certain the North Vietnamese were trying to embarrass him and his father by getting him to accept an early release. As punishment for this defiance, just before the summer of 1968, McCain's cellmate, Bud Day, was moved to another cell. McCain was then placed in solitary confinement, where he would remain for the next two years.

During his time in solitary confinement, McCain kept his morale intact by insulting the guards and getting smashed around by them. These small acts of rebellion made him feel as if he were at least doing something. The worst of his guards would kick him when he was down, in the head and sometimes in the leg, but not his bad leg. McCain felt he was still being treated as the son of an admiral and wasn't receiving the kind of pummeling he had previously suffered.

McCain continued to refuse early release. He explained to his captors that POW protocol states that prisoners should be released in the order they are captured, and McCain knew he wasn't next. North Vietnamese Major Dai, who was called "the Cat," pushed for McCain to return home, citing medical reasons. But these were partially invented, as the medical damage was already done, and so McCain continued to refuse release.

Death Before Dishonor?

McCain waited, expecting the harsh treatment to return. It took a week, which was a kind of torture in itself. When it came, the most brutal of his captors led his men in a terrible beating, asking McCain to admit to his war crimes. McCain refused, and the guards moved to a torture called the ropes. The American's arms were tied behind his back, then further lashed together and kept that way all night. During the day,

he was beaten. He was given some water after a couple of days and then suffered from dysentery, an infection that causes severe diarrhea. He could barely move and didn't always make it to the bucket provided to go to the bathroom. This was repeated day after day, night after night.

McCain held out for a week before he said he was ready to admit, to "confess," to war crimes. He felt as though he were behaving dishonorably, that he had been broken, the one thing the McCain family despised. McCain tried to write the confession, keeping it obvious that it was forced. In *Faith of My Fathers*, he revisited his writing: "I am a black criminal . . . I performed the deeds of an air pirate. I almost died and the Vietnamese people saved my life." Despondent after signing, he went back to his cell and almost succeeded in hanging himself from the bars of his window, but guards rushed in and stopped him. He wasn't left alone for days afterward. McCain was at his lowest point, feeling he let his fellow POWs down. He didn't know that most of them had signed similar statements, some after fewer days of torture. When asked about it later, McCain said, "I

In April 2000, McCain returned to Hoa Lo Prison (the "Hanoi Hilton") with his son Jack. McCain has said that he is no longer angry with his former captors.

still believe I failed . . . I'm convinced I did the best that I could, but the best that I could wasn't good enough."

Christmas, at Home and in Hanoi

Meanwhile, at home, wife Carol was in a devastating car accident. After she delivered presents to a friend's house on Christmas Eve 1969, her car slipped on the icy road and crashed into a telephone pole. She was thrown out of the car into the snow, lying there until police found her. At the hospital, Carol was unable to communicate, but she could hear doctors discussing whether or not to amputate her leg. Fortunately, she kept her leg, but she needed to spend six months in the hospital. (Between the accident and the end of 1971, she would undergo twenty-three operations.) When she finally left the hospital, she was four inches shorter and needed crutches, but she forbade people to tell her husband, not wanting him to have one more thing to worry about during his captivity.

After thirty-one months in solitary confinement, around Christmas 1970, McCain was transferred to a prison called Camp Unity. His old cellmate Bud Day was there, along with forty-nine other American soldiers. McCain had great opportunity now to bond with these men, improve his morale, and exercise to heal some of his physical issues. The soldiers kept up their spirits by holding classes for each other, singing when they could, and exercising. The guards still punished and beat them, but at least they were together.

In March 1973, after U.S. secretary of state Henry Kissinger signed the peace agreement with the North Vietnamese, McCain was freed. Along with the other prisoners of war, he left Vietnam on an American transport plane, five and a half years after his fighter plane had gone down.

March 14, 1973—Following McCain's release, Lieutenant Commander Jay Coupe Jr. escorts the former POW to Hanoi's Gia Lam Airport.

Without a doubt, the strength of character and physical endurance McCain built over those years were formative. A somewhat insolent and green John McCain flew into Vietnam, and a more mature, war-weary John McCain flew out.

FOUR

A War Veteran Comes Home

McCain's release from the North Vietnamese was heralded by the American press. The former POW was flown in a huge C-141 transport plane to the Island of Luzon, in the Republic of the Philippines to spend a few days at Clark Air Base, where medical experts examined him. He also talked to his wife Carol and first learned of her injuries, telling her that he didn't look so great himself. McCain read and read, having missed five and a half years of history— including John F. Kennedy and Martin Luther King's assassinations, Richard Nixon's rise to the presidency, and the moon landing of *Apollo 11*.

Home Is Where the Heart Is

From Clark Air Base, McCain was flown home for the reunion with his family. McCain, Carol, and their son Doug—who was fourteen years old and had been injured in a soccer match—were all on crutches. This brought a moment of humor to the meeting and the media photos that followed. It was a happy time. First, the entire family reunited. Later, when McCain and his wife spent time alone, he was able to tell Carol everything. In an article written soon after for *U.S. News and World Report*, McCain noted, "I had a lot of time to think over there, and I came to the conclusion that one of the most important things in life—along with a man's family—is to make some contribution to his country." During the next few years, he would continue to serve in the navy.

The time spent in prison, an unimaginable ordeal, made McCain stronger. In addition, it distinguished him from his father and grandfather and forged in him a special kind of confidence. McCain searched out his old teacher, William Ravenel, for he remembered how his teacher believed in him

Less than a week after leaving Vietnam, McCain is reunited with his family at the Naval Air Station in Jacksonville, Florida.

and wanted to talk about his experiences, especially his refusal for early release. He was sure Ravenel would understand. McCain was very disappointed to learn that Ravenel had died, at age fifty-one, two years before McCain was released.

From 1973 through 1977, McCain underwent intensive physical therapy, including a three-month hospital stay to focus on his injuries. (To this day, he cannot lift his arms above his chest.) He also met with navy psychologists, who concluded that McCain's time as a POW had somehow freed him from the shadow of his famous father and grandfather. McCain did feel different, but he was still determined to continue serving his country. So, he took a job as the commander of the Replacement Air Group (RAG) 174, in Jacksonville, Florida. There, he trained carrier pilots and crews in what was then the navy's biggest squadron. He found his teaching style to be like that of Lieutenant Commander Ferrell: some yelling and then more patient explanation. This was the first commanding position McCain held, and the squadron flourished, even winning an award for excellence.

Lieutenant Commander John McCain greets President Richard M. Nixon, in May 1973. Injuries sustained in captivity required McCain to use crutches for months following his release.

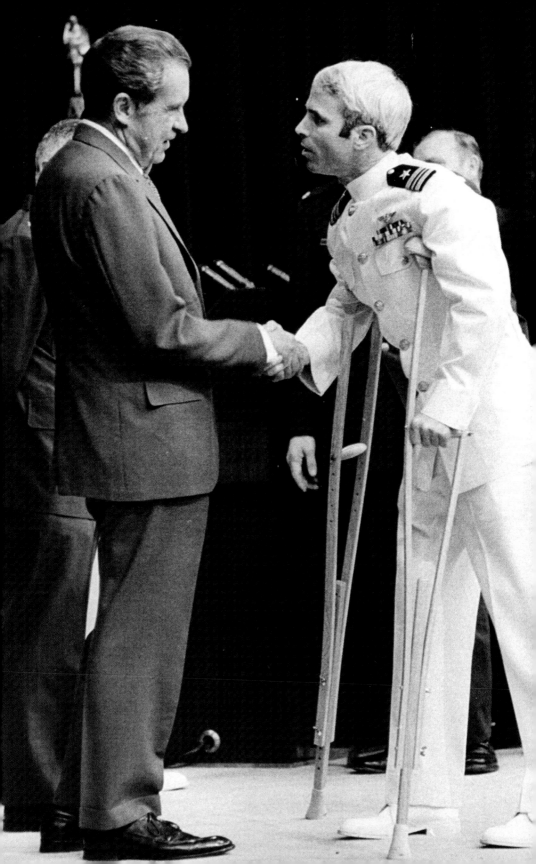

The Navy's Liaison to Congress

When John McCain was attending Annapolis, his father Jack served as the navy's senior liaison officer to Congress. In this capacity, Jack McCain helped expand the liaison's position, working with congressional lobbyists and others who were politically connected. Twenty years later, Jack's son was assigned to the same office. After McCain's tour in Jacksonville ended, the chief of naval operations, Admiral James Holloway, looked for a position that would suit McCain and make use of his name and his talents. Holloway chose the liaison post, and McCain became second in command. Within a few months, McCain was the senior advisor.

From 1977 to 1981, McCain, served as the navy liaison to Congress. The position entailed representing the navy in all dealings with the Senate and senators, planning trips, and accompanying senators abroad. At this point, the personality McCain had inherited from his mother dominated—he was gregarious and socially capable. His command positions ensured that he could run a squadron or an office. McCain was often described as funny, and his office became a gathering place. He counted among his friends senators Gary Hart, John Tower, and William Cohen.

As congressional liaison, McCain grew accustomed to mixing with the rich and powerful. In this photo from May 1978, he chats easily with Ronald and Nancy Reagan, the future president and first lady, and popular actor Michael Landon.

The social side of politics came easily for McCain, as he had seen how his parents entertained many politicians during his father's tenure as navy liaison and congressional lobbyist.

As liaison, McCain was not afraid to challenge the decisions being made at the highest levels of government, especially when it came to issues about which he felt strongly. In 1978, for example, the administration of President Jimmy Carater planned to replace the USS *Midway* with a smaller aircraft carrier. McCain believed passionately that this would be a mistake, and he lobbied to replace the *Midway* instead with a super-carrier. The navy accepted the president's decision, but McCain could not. He respectfully explained his opinion on the subject, working behind the scenes with Senator Jim McGovern to disseminate information about the need for the super-carrier, the need to keep the navy strong.

Although President Carter vetoed the bill the first year, McCain and retired rear admiral Mark Hill continued to lobby senators, and the next year the bill was approved. This was a rare event in Washington. This was also McCain's last big battle as navy liaison. He had worked hard, enjoyed success, and developed a taste for more. Working with senators showed McCain the power they held. Being friends with them showed McCain they were people, just like him. The navy wasn't going to make him an admiral like his father and grandfather had been (the only father-son set to achieve that rank), and McCain wanted more.

But on the Home Front . . .

McCain was tasting success in Washington, but at the same time, his marriage to Carol started to fall apart. In the past, they had separated a few times, and McCain admitted that he had been unfaithful.

But this time, they had both changed so much that it was impossible to sustain the relationship. In 1980, he and Carol divorced, and he willingly gave his wife a very generous settlement. She retained custody of the children, who by then were thirteen, seventeen, and nineteen years old. Later in 1980, McCain married Cindy Hensley, an heiress to a sizeable fortune and a resident of Arizona, the state in which McCain would begin his career as an elected politician.

Setting Up in the Southwest

The newlyweds set up house in hot and sunny Phoenix, Arizona. McCain went to work for his new father-in-law, as the vice president of public relations department of his company, an Anheuser-Busch distributor. James Hensley had many connections, and traveling around the state, McCain met people and made observations about his new home.

McCain was preparing himself as if he were interested in a future as an elected politician, which is exactly what he was doing. Friends remember that he hinted at a Senate seat while he was still in Washington, but even brash McCain couldn't run for senator without holding any other elected position first. McCain was usually impulsive, but his advisors

encouraged him to slow down, not announce his intentions, and just get to know people in power in the state. Arizona was a good place for McCain to run, as the population had increased tremendously over the past decade and was gaining an extra congressional seat. Luckily, John Rhodes, the congressman from Arizona's First District, announced his retirement. Coincidentally, the McCains bought a house in the First District. Things were falling into place.

As his campaign to win the Republican congressional primary began in earnest, McCain started meeting his constituents. (Primaries are the elections that determine which candidates represent their parties in the general election.) McCain was running against fellow Republican Jim Mack. At first, as McCain went door to door, people thought he was a salesman. But eventually the word spread and people were excited to meet him. McCain might have been new to Arizona, but so were many of the other residents. McCain had a brash quality and a confidence that went over well with voters. He had his own money and raised even more money to

May 17, 1980—Forty-three-year-old John McCain weds second wife Cindy Hensley in Phoenix, Arizona. The couple had been introduced at a military reception in Hawaii.

spend on his campaign, and his television ads were slick, making the most of his Washington connections and POW history.

Still, McCain had to fight accusations that he was just using Arizona for personal gain, that he was merely a carpetbagger. To silence these charges, McCain had a clever reply. As Robert Timberg wrote in *John McCain, An American Odyssey*, McCain finally said to his constituents: "I spent twenty-two years in the Navy. My father was in the Navy. My grandfather was in the Navy . . . I wish I could have had the luxury, like you, of growing up and living and spending my entire life in a nice place like the First District of Arizona, but I was doing other things . . . As a matter of fact, when I think about it now, the place I lived the longest in my life was Hanoi." After playing his war hero card, the carpetbagger issue plagued him no more.

In the Republican primary, McCain received 32 percent of the votes—more than any other candidate—to win by a plurality. He then easily won the general election over Democrat William Hegarty. In the new year, McCain would be off to Washington, and his long career in the Congress would begin.

The Republican Party in 1980

In the 1980s, the Republican Party was strong under conservative Republican president Ronald Reagan. The country had two major concerns— restoring economic prosperity and fighting the global spread of Communism—that played to conservative Republican strengths. Reagan's administration successfully lowered taxes to encourage people to spend more, which jump-started the economy. And when it came to national defense, the United States developed a huge nuclear arsenal and seemed prepared to use it against the primary enemy, the former United Soviet Socialist Republic.

In the early 1980s, the Republican Party viewed McCain favorably. He seemed like a good conservative Republican, one who wouldn't make trouble. This was true, to an extent, but McCain wasn't afraid to speak out against his party when he thought it was necessary. In 1983, for example, only ten months into his tenure as congressman, he had the courage to go against his party leadership. President Reagan was faced with an unstable Lebanon, in the Middle East. Reagan had marines stationed in Beirut, the Lebanese capital, and offshore. When the House of Representatives was to vote on whether

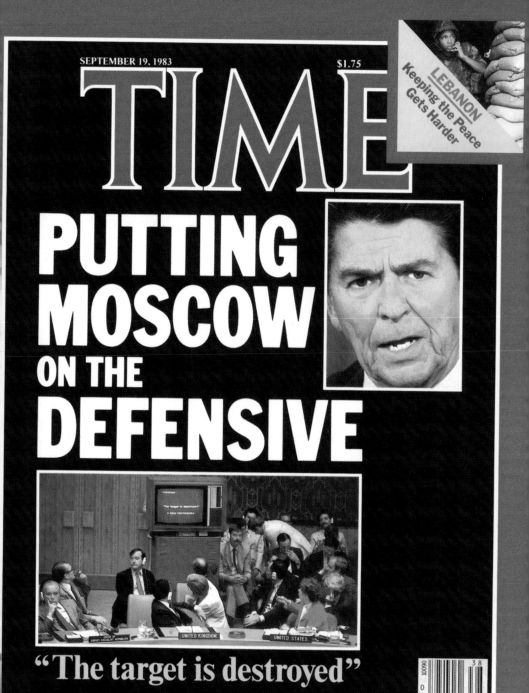

SEPTEMBER 19, 1983 $1.75

TIME

LEBANON
Keeping the Peace
Gets Harder

PUTTING MOSCOW ON THE DEFENSIVE

UNITED KINGDOM   UNITED STATES

"The target is destroyed"

The cover of *Time* magazine from September 1983 underscores the global political challenges facing the first-term congressman. The following month, Lebanon would erupt in chaos.

American troops would remain there for another eighteen months, Reagan urged them to keep the marines in position. But McCain strongly felt that the military presence was a mistake. He questioned the purpose of troops offshore and wondered if the United States would really go to fight for Lebanon if the situation escalated. Having seen a similar situation in Vietnam, McCain was not ready to send U.S. soldiers into battle. An article in *Rolling Stone* magazine commended him, saying, "It takes enormous courage for an old military man to deliver a message like that." Republicans, especially those in Phoenix, weren't happy that McCain voted against the proposal. Unfortunately, it took a disaster to show that McCain's view was the right one. On October 23, 1983, a suicide bomber demolished barracks in Beirut, killing 220 marines, eighteen members of the navy, and three army soldiers.

Congressman McCain was building momentum. He had promised to spend every weekend home, in Arizona, and during his first year, he managed to spend almost all of his weekends with his constituents, attending parades, appearing at local events, and holding meetings. All this time spent in his home state ensured that his reputation remained positive. In 1984, McCain ran unchallenged for the Republican nomination, winning the general election against Democrat Harry Braun with 78 percent of the vote. McCain would represent his state in the House of Representatives for another two years, and then he would make yet another great leap forward.

FIVE

THE SENATOR FROM ARIZONA

In the introduction to his book
Character Is Destiny, McCain wrote:
"The best I can claim for my own
character is that it is still, even at this
late date, a work in progress . . . But
were I to use my own character as
an example of how to build yours, I
would lack one of the most important
qualities of good character—honesty.
My own children, who have suffered,
as they often remind me, considerable
embarrassment already from their
father's public and unconvincing
attempts at proving himself a role
model for the young, have taught me
just enough humility to avoid that
conceit."

Race for the Senate

In 1986, McCain ran for the Senate seat vacated by Barry Goldwater, a widely respected politician known for speaking his mind. For years, Goldwater was seen as the quintessential conservative Republican—against taxes and federal involvement in daily life, and strongly opposed to Communism.

McCain was a fitting candidate to fill Goldwater's seat, and for a long time he had no opponent. A little over a year before election day, however, Richard Kimball entered the race. A thirty-seven-year-old former member of the Arizona Corporation Commission, Kimball trailed McCain in the polls for months. Then, in June, people working with Kimball found tapes of a speech McCain had made to students at the University of Arizona in which McCain joked about a retirement community he had recently spoken at, called Leisure World. Instead, he insensitively referred to it as "Seizure World." Piling on the criticism, Kimball also called into question the ability of McCain to represent the interests of normal Arizonans when most of the funds McCain had raised came from such "special-interest" groups as defense contractors, utility and petroleum companies, and real estate investors.

Instead of giving a general explanation, McCain defensively called Kimball's campaign "one of the most sloppy and dirty campaigns in Arizona history." McCain was learning something about political races—he couldn't avoid direct questions. He looked bad at this point, and he wasn't coming up with anything to satisfy the public. The Arizona press was pushing McCain in the papers, but it wasn't enough. Kimball was challenging him to debates that McCain's advisors made him avoid, and the former boxer was getting restless. Still, the usually impulsive McCain waited until, finally, the two candidates agreed to a televised debate in October. McCain was drilled by his handlers, who

What Does a Senator Do?

Every state elects two senators who are responsible for representing them in the U.S. Senate. Throughout their six-year terms, senators write and vote on bills that come before Congress. All bills must pass the Senate before they can go to the president to be signed into law. Senators spend most of their time in Washington, but when the Senate is not in session, they usually spend time in their home states, gathering information and ideas to bring back to Washington, D.C.

helped him to develop solid answers to all the possible insults and accusations Kimball might resort to in the debate.

At the debate site, McCain's people made one change, putting a riser underneath the five-foot-nine McCain to counteract a camera angle that would have made him appear even shorter. McCain—calm, cool, and collected—clearly emerged victorious. Kimball had a holier-than-thou attitude and was described as seeming angry. He even mentioned McCain's height enhancer, but McCain didn't take the bait. Kimball finished by telling people why they shouldn't vote for McCain, and McCain finished by telling people why they should. Two weeks later, McCain won the election with 60 percent of the vote. He had joined the ranks of those he worked with when he was navy liaison. Finally, as one of Arizona's senators, he would be able to make major decisions that influenced the country and the military.

Political Scandal: The Keating Five

McCain was friendly with a man named Charles Keating III, whose company ran a savings and loan— a type of bank—in Arizona. The two former pilots met at a navy dinner in 1981, and McCain and wife

President George H. W. Bush *(right)* re-enacts John McCain's 1987 Senate swearing-in ceremony, with wife, Cindy, and their children in attendance.

Cindy even went on a few vacations to Keating's house in the Bahamas.

In 1987, Keating's huge savings and loan (or S&L) was failing. It had given out too many high-risk loans on which borrowers were defaulting, and its practices were being reviewed by regulators, government officials who investigated the nation's hundreds of failing savings and loans. Keating thought the regulators were being particularly hard on him, and he needed more time to make back the money he had lost. He called on his friends in the Senate for

help. Senator Dennis DeConcini, the other senator from Arizona and a Democrat, asked McCain to attend a meeting with the federal regulators. McCain, thinking there was no reason to meet, declined, much to Keating's annoyance.

Within the next two months, though, McCain came to think that the regulators might be unfairly scrutinizing Keating. As Keating was an influential constituent, McCain finally scheduled the meetings. The first was held in Senator DeConcini's office on April 2, along with senators Alan Cranston (a Democrat from California) and John Glenn (a Democrat from Ohio). DeConcini asked regulator Edward Gray, the chairman of the Federal Home Loan Bank Board, to go easy on Keating. But Gray refused, saying that he was part of the big picture and not interested in the individual companies at all.

On April 9, Senators McCain, Glenn, DiConcini, and Cranston were joined for the second meeting by Senator Don Riegle, a Democrat from Michigan. (In the media, the group would be called the Keating Five.) They met with William Black, the deputy

In a subdued atmosphere, senators involved in the Keating Five scandal, along with their attorneys, follow testimony in a Senate Ethics Committee hearing.

What Happened to the Savings and Loans?

Savings and loans (S&Ls) were financial institutions that allowed people to open savings accounts and offered loans to others, using the savings of the initial investors. Throughout history, S&Ls had strict regulations. In the 1980s, the regulations were relaxed on the kinds of loans S&Ls were allowed to offer, and many S&Ls then grew bigger. In addition, the loan limit was raised from $40,000 to $100,000. Since the government insured S&L loans through the Federal Savings and Loan Insurance Corporation (FSLIC), raising the limit also increased the amount federal insurance would have to cover in case an S&L failed.

Many owners of S&Ls took advantage of the new rules. They gave loans to commercial clients (who were less likely than private borrowers to be able to pay them back), and they invested the S&Ls' money in riskier ventures, many of which went bankrupt. The combination of deregulation and increase in insurance led many S&L managers to take risks with the money they were supposed to manage. Some invested in new construction that never fulfilled expectations, thus losing their clients' money and costing the government billions, as the bank customers collected on the FSLIC insurance.

director of the Federal Savings and Loan Insurance Corporation, along with other officials. According to Black's notes, McCain started the meeting by saying, "One of our jobs as elected officials is to help

Embattled financier Charles Keating is sworn in during the House Banking Committee hearing on the failure of his Lincoln Savings and Loan Association.

constituents in a proper fashion . . . ACC [American Continental Corp., Keating's company] is a big employer and important to the local economy. I wouldn't want any special favors for them . . . I don't want any part of our conversation to be improper." Black's careful note-taking during the meeting actually proved to be good for McCain, who was eventually cleared of most wrongdoing by the Senate Ethics Committee appointed to investigate.

Senator DeConcini, who had much more involvement with Keating, bore the brunt of the responsibility. McCain went on record saying that he attended the meetings because Keating was a constituent asking his senators for assistance. That was too gentle a spin. In October 1989, an investigation by the media unearthed documents showing that three years earlier, Cindy McCain and her father had invested $359,100 in a Keating shopping center. The Bahamas trips that McCain and his family took with Keating were also revealed, though McCain had paid for some of them and not others. In addition, it came out that Keating had contributed thousands of dollars to McCain's political campaigns. This was a troubling time for McCain.

Redemption in Washington, D.C.

The Senate Ethics Committee finally reached a decision in November 1989. Robert Bennett was lead counsel. DeConcini, who didn't seek reelection in 1994, was held the most culpable. Of McCain, Bennett commented, "In the case of Senator McCain, there is very substantial evidence that he thought he had an understanding with Senator DeConcini's office that certain matters would not be gone into at the meeting with Chairman Gray . . . Moreover, there is substantial evidence that, as a result of Senator McCain's refusal to do certain things, he had a fallout with Mr. Keating." The committee gently admonished McCain and cleared Senator Glenn. McCain's final comment on the Keating scandal wrapped up another chapter in his life in which he was able to admit mistakes and move forward: "I was judged eventually, after three years, of using, quote, poor judgment, and I agree with that assessment." McCain was reelected to the Senate in 1992, with an overwhelming majority of the vote.

Party Spending and Pork Barrels

In 1994, McCain and Wisconsin Democratic senator Russ Feingold took on the issue of corruption in campaign financing. In particular, they wanted to ban "soft" money contributions. "Hard" money describes funds contributed directly to an individual politician; these funds are disclosed to the public and limited by legislation. "Soft" money, on the other hand, describes contributions made to political parties; these contributions could be unlimited, potentially giving politicians with rich contributors an unfair advantage.

For their efforts, in 1999, McCain and Feingold shared the tenth John F. Kennedy Profile in Courage

Senators McCain and Feingold march with Doris Haddock in Washington, D.C. Haddock, an elderly New Hampshire native, walked across the United States in support of campaign finance reform.

Award. At the award ceremony, Caroline Kennedy said McCain and Feingold "defied the extraordinary pressures of partisan politics and special interests and stood up for what they felt was best for the country. In doing so, they suffered the displeasure of their party leaders and key constituency groups and even risked reelection to office. In a time when politics and government have been marked by incivility and partisanship, these senators distinguished themselves by their political courage and by their vision of what was right for the country." The McCain-Feingold Bill, now called the Bipartisan Campaign Reform Act, became law in 2002.

In addition to campaign finance reform, McCain also stood with Senator Feingold in opposition to pork barrel spending. This is money for "pet projects" that senators add to the appropriations bills that authorize the government to spend federal money. Throughout the 1990s and into the 2000s, McCain regularly called attention to projects that he thought were the worst examples of pork. Unfortunately, he and Feingold were in the minority on this issue, as most other senators found it very valuable politically to deliver federal money for projects in their home states.

In other ways, too, Senator McCain continued to establish his reputation as a leader in Washington,

September 27, 1999—An animated McCain announces he will run for the Republican nomination in the 2000 presidential election. Wife Cindy and their adopted daughter, Bridget, look on.

especially regarding military issues. In 1999, for example, President Bill Clinton wanted to use high-flying planes to bomb Serbians, who were involved in "ethnic cleansing," in Kosovo. McCain spoke up, presenting a better strategy that was ultimately successful. He pushed for more ground troops and lower-flying combat missions, which would help protect innocent civilians.

An Eventful Decade

McCain's personal life, like his political one, had its ups and downs in the 1990s. One of the high points came in 1992, when the McCains adopted a daughter, Bridget, from a Bangladeshi orphanage. On the down side, Cindy struggled with addiction to prescription pain medication, and McCain was treated for skin cancer. McCain is used to weathering tough moments, and the family came through these challenges with their heads held high. Sometimes criticized for being absent at some functions, Cindy McCain purposely stays out of the spotlight, prefer-ring to be home raising their children rather than out at political events. McCain's next move, though, wouldn't allow her to remain on the sidelines for long.

SIX

ROAD TO THE PRESIDENCY?

Not long ago, John McCain told *Men's Journal* magazine that presidential ambition is "a disease that can only be cured by embalming fluid." McCain wants to be president; he has wanted to be president for many years.

In 1999, McCain published a book called *Faith of My Fathers*, which covered half his life story, from birth through his release from the POW camp. His closing line in the book was, "I held on to the memory, left the bad behind, and moved on." It was true. McCain had managed to parlay his navy career into a stint as congressman, ultimately becoming a

U.S. senator. All of this prepared him for a run at the presidency.

The first step on that journey to the presidency is winning your party's nomination. This means that you have to win the majority of delegates in the primaries. The delegates vote for the candidate, and the candidate with the most votes wins the nomination.

Straight Talk Express

Early in 2000, McCain's campaign got off to a great start. McCain's book, written with Mark Salter, was well received by the public. People lined up at bookstores for readings and autographed copies. For someone kicking off a campaign for president, it was terrific. He was a war hero, congressman, senator, and now celebrated author.

Showing that he had learned from mistakes in his Arizona campaigns, McCain called his campaign bus the Straight Talk Express. He and his political advisers built his reputation on the principle that he would give people a straight answer to any question asked. His energy and charisma shone through as he appeared on television and gave numerous print interviews.

McCain focused on the issues that had always been important to him: reducing pork barrel spending

C
A
R
E
E
R

P
R
O
F
I
L
E
S

January 7, 2000—McCain *(far right)* chats with reporters as they travel aboard McCain's campaign bus, the Straight Talk Express.

and putting government money to better use. He spoke out against additional tax cuts when the national debt was huge. Democrats could relate to these ideas, and Independents recognized that the senator was not a "pure" Republican, which made McCain more viable to them. But McCain first had to secure the support of the nation's Republicans.

Republicans typically emphasize keeping the government out of the personal life of the average American. They prefer lower taxes, and when tax revenue is raised, they prefer to see it spent on corporate welfare or military programs. Democrats, on the other hand, believe strongly in raising money through taxes to fund social programs they think will help the American people. In 2000, however, the U.S. economy was strong, and the

CAREER PROFILES

question of what to do with tax money was not a burning issue.

A Rift Within the Republican Party

In contrast to the 1980s, Republicans in 2000 were much more concerned with the "culture war" than with national security or economic reform. Abortion, as an example, is a huge battle in the culture war. Most abortion foes are conservative Republicans. McCain, when asked what he would do if his teenage daughter became pregnant, staked out a middle ground. He made it clear that he would counsel her and hope she had the child, but the final decision would be hers. In early 2000, such messages didn't always sit right with many Republican voters who wanted their leaders to support their beliefs with greater conviction.

McCain was proposing higher taxes on wealthier Americans and possible tax breaks for people such as single mothers. Also, everyone knew that McCain wanted to limit the power and influence of corporate and big money interests in American politics. This

Campaigning for the Republican nomination, John McCain speaks from the steps of the Alpha Delta fraternity at Dartmouth College. Amusingly, the Alpha Delta house was the inspiration for the movie *Animal House*.

left most Republicans across the nation unexcited about John McCain. Instead, they liked what they were hearing from the other real contender for the nomination, Texas governor George W. Bush. Bush had a lot more money to spend and had many capable political advisors helping him craft his message and get it out to the voters. However, McCain had money of his own, was raising more, and was already very accessible to the media. It was shaping up to be a tight race.

Early in his campaign, McCain ran into trouble with the Christian Right when he alienated two influential Christian evangelists, Jerry Falwell and Pat Robertson. McCain called these men "agents of intolerance" and accused them of focusing more on political and financial gain than helping people gain salvation. While McCain was making enemies among the evangelists, George W. Bush was playing up his status as a born-again Christian and invoking Christ's name in his speeches.

The first presidential primary is held in New Hampshire, with the winner there almost always going on to win the party nomination. In New Hampshire, where Republicans tend to be rather moderate, McCain was looking forward to the national election, sending out a message that would

Both Pat Robertson *(top)* and Jerry Falwell *(bottom)* opposed John McCain's presidential candidacy, citing differences on religious and moral issues.

attract all types of voters. He gained momentum by speaking to Republican audiences of a new "McCain majority" that would bring in and encompass Independents and Democrats, too. McCain's momentum carried him through—he clobbered Bush, winning 49 percent of the vote to Bush's 30 percent. Things were looking very good for the senator from Arizona as the campaigns headed into the next big event, the South Carolina Republican primary.

Three Weeks Can Be a Long Time

During the three weeks between New Hampshire and the second primary in South Carolina, McCain tried to keep the conversation focused on the issues. But since there was so little difference between him and Bush on many of the issues, the campaigning was bound to turn personal. In the end, McCain wasn't prepared for the barrage of negative campaigning launched by the Bush camp. The population of South Carolina is predominantly conservative and Christian, and McCain would need all the help he could get to beat the born-again Bush. Instead of riding the momentum from New Hampshire, however, McCain's campaign fell apart.

Publicly, Bush relied on typical political maneuvers, like painting McCain as being too liberal. But some aspects of the South Carolina primary indicated that people supporting Bush were engaged in a behind-the-scenes smear campaign against McCain. For example, before the primary vote, some anonymous "push pollers" telephoned McCain supporters to ask if they would be more or less likely to vote for McCain if they knew he had fathered an illegitimate child who was black. The polling had no basis in fact, but in conservative, Christian South Carolina, it raised questions about McCain's character.

John McCain and Representative Lindsey Graham *(right)* campaign door-to-door in South Carolina, where McCain ran into political trouble in 2000.

CAREER PROFILES

A follow-up blow came from a professor at Bob Jones University, a conservative South Carolina school that had given George W. Bush a warm welcome when he spoke prior to the primary. In an e-mail sent around the state, professor Richard Hand wrote that McCain "chose to sire children without marriage." This was a false reference to McCain's adopted daughter, who being from Bangladesh has a darker complexion than the rest of her family. Bush denied any connection to the rumor mill and commented that he deplored negative campaigning, but the damage had already been done. Bush beat McCain by a wide margin in South Carolina.

A Downhill Road

Early in March 2000, McCain was attacked in television advertisements by a small Republican organization called the Republicans for Clean Air Committee. McCain told people at a rally on Wall Street, "Don't be fooled by them, my friends. Don't let the special interests decide who's going to win this election . . . Somebody's putting in $2 million to try to hijack the campaign here in New York," pointing a finger at the Bush campaign. He continued, "This is what I've been fighting against . . . this soft money, nobody knows where it comes from." In fact, McCain filed a federal complaint a few days later when it was learned that two brothers, Texas billionaires Charles and Sam Wyly, had organized the company and the ads. The Republicans for Clean Air Committee wasn't a real committee—just a name on paperwork. Eventually, McCain would rally against such 527 groups, as they are known, for being allowed to operate with little to no government oversight.

Not-So-Super Tuesday

Super Tuesday, March 7, 2000, was a day of eleven primaries (California, Connecticut, Georgia, Maine, Maryland, Massachusetts, Missouri, New York, Ohio, Rhode Island, and Vermont) and one caucus (Minnesota). Up to that date, McCain had won seven primaries and Bush had won eleven. Unfortunately, on Super Tuesday, the negative cam-paigning, defending, and smearing finally caught up with McCain: He lost in all states except for Connecticut, Massachusetts, Rhode Island and Vermont. Republicans clearly weren't voting for McCain, and two days later he pulled out of the race. "I've been in my country's service since I was seventeen years old," he said in a speech to his supporters. "I neither know nor want any other life, for I can find no greater honor than service.

You served your country in this campaign by fighting for the causes that will sustain America's greatness. Keep fighting. America needs you. I ask from you one last promise: Promise me that you will never give up, that you will continue your service in the worthy cause of revitalizing our democracy. Thank you." McCain, a little wiser, returned to his full-time job as a U.S. senator.

McCain and the War in Iraq

In 2003, the United States invaded Iraq to depose dictator Saddam Hussein. The war, which Senator McCain wholly supported, helped to bring together the various elements of his Republican Party. By the 2004 presidential campaign, McCain had strategically mended ties with George W. Bush. (There was no doubt that Bush, who was still relatively popular at the time, would be the Republican candidate for president.) Despite his loss in the presidential primary of 2000, McCain was still hugely popular in his state, and in 2004, he was reelected to the Senate with 77 percent of the vote.

Support for the war in Iraq is something McCain dealt with frequently. He said often that there was a need to go to war, but in 2006, he began saying publicly that he would have made different decisions along the way. As the security situation in Iraq has worsened, McCain has spoken out more critically against the war there. For instance, in an interview on MSNBC in August 2006, he criticized the Bush administration for leading the American people into thinking the mission in Iraq would be "some kind of day at the beach." McCain said if he were president he would "listen very carefully to his military com-manders" in the field. In an interview with Katie Couric, he said, "Mistakes have been made."

Related to the war on terror, McCain has been active on issues regarding the interrogation of prisoners of war and terror suspects. This is a topic that has been under discussion since the first arrests were made, soon after September 11, 2001. In 2006, the guidelines of the Geneva Convention were challenged by the Bush administration, and McCain, along with Senators John Warner (Republican, Virginia) and Lindsey Graham (Republican, South Carolina), worked hard to oppose Bush's push to allow harsher interrogation of terror suspects.

In the global war on terror, the Bush administration pushed for more flexibility with terror suspects, saying the Geneva Convention was outdated for this new type of war against a stateless enemy. McCain had other beliefs, asserting that once the United States

April 2004—An Iraqi detainee suspected of being an insurgent militiaman awaits interrogation. As a former prisoner of war, McCain is a supporter of the Geneva Convention, which extends certain rights to POWs.

starts interpreting the rules, other parties can interpret them as well. McCain, with Graham and Warner, put forward ideas to clarify the law so that terror suspects are interrogated humanely and in accordance with the Geneva Convention. They proposed clearly outlining, in U.S. law, what a "grave breach" of Article Three it would be, allowing the Central Intelligence Agency (CIA) and military personnel to interrogate suspects without breaking the rules.

McCain has his own experience to support his opinion—he was tortured to the breaking point twice but never told his captors anything the least bit helpful. In September 2006, McCain, Graham, and Warner all voted in favor of the bill that came before the Senate, claiming that their concerns had been addressed. Even so, many saw this battle as a loss for McCain, since the final bill gives the president of the United States authorization to define the terms of the Geneva Convention.

Republicans Take a Thumping

In the mid-term elections of 2006, American voters displayed frustration with the deteriorating conditions in Iraq and the lack of common-sense leadership among the ruling Republicans. In the end, large numbers of Republicans were voted out of office, and Democrats took control of both the Senate and the House of Representatives.

The Republicans were reeling, so a week after the voting, on November 11, McCain tried to rally his party. Addressing members of GOPAC, a powerful Republican political action committee, McCain reminded them that it was not the Republican principles the voters rejected but the Republican politicians who valued their power more than the principles of "common-sense conservatism."

Common-sense conservatives, he said in his speech, "believe in a short list of self-evident truths: love of country; respect for our unique influence on history; a strong defense and strong alliances based on mutual respect and mutual responsibility; steadfast opposition to threats to our security and values that matches resources to ends wisely; and confident, reliable, consistent leadership to advance human rights, democracy, peace, and security." McCain's speech was warmly applauded, and a week later, the Arizona senator announced the formation of an exploratory committee, essentially announcing his candidacy for the 2008 presidential elections.

What Is in Store for 2008?

A politician needs to define his positions on practically every issue in order to win an election, so McCain was very vocal with his opinions and worked hard to keep himself in the spotlight through the end of 2006. He stood strong on certain issues and reevaluated others, positioning himself to elicit the most support. While some criticized his shifts in allegiance or changes of heart, he attributes his evolution to his maturing and to a better understanding of the issues. His changing didn't sit well with some, but these people don't realize that politicians need to work together with different kinds of people to achieve goals. It would be self-defeating for McCain to remain stagnant or sever ties with everyone he has ever disagreed with.

McCain positioned himself for a presidential run in other ways, too. His political action committee, called Straight Talk America, hired Terry Nelson, who was national political director for President Bush's 2004 campaign. He built alliances with other politicians (even ones with whom he does not see eye to eye on every issue), and he had campaigned for many Republicans who ran in the November 2006 mid-term elections, laying a base of support for his future presidential race.

McCain knows he will be facing a field of other skillful politicians campaigning hard against him. Perhaps more daunting, he will be facing a country

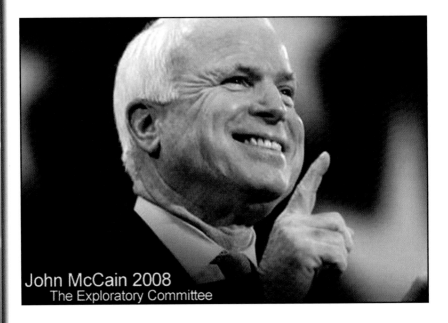

John McCain 2008
The Exploratory Committee

John McCain's photo from the Web site he created to explore running for president in 2008: www.ExploreMcCain.com

of people who are, in his words, angry about government spending and who are expecting reforms in immigration, campaign finance, lobbying, and leadership ethics. But he seemed unfazed by the challenges ahead. After all, from the schoolyards of his childhood to the prison camps of Vietnam to the chambers of Congress, John McCain has never been one to back down from a fight.

1936 John Sidney McCain III born in Coco Solo, Panama Canal Zone, Panama.

1954 Graduates from Episcopal High School, in Alexandria, Virginia.

1958 Graduates from the U.S. Naval Academy, at Annapolis, Maryland.

1958–1960 Trains to be a navy pilot.

1960–1964 Carrier pilot on the USS *Intrepid* and the USS *Enterprise*.

1965 Marries Carol Shepp.

1967 Survives an explosion on the USS *Forrestal*.

1967–1973 Shot down over Hanoi, Vietnam; held as POW.

1974 Attends National War College, in Washington, D.C.

1977–1981 Serves as the U.S. Navy's liaison officer to the U.S. Senate.

1980 Marries Cindy Lou Hensley.

1981 Works in public relations for father-in-law's beer distributorship.

1982 Elected congressman from Arizona.

1987 Elected U.S. senator from Arizona.

1989 McCain implicated in Keating scandal.

1991 Cleared by Senate Ethics Committee in Keating scandal.

1992 Re-elected to the Senate.

2000 Withdraws from the Republican presidential primary.

2004 Reelected to the Senate.

2006 Announces he will run for U.S. president.

GLOSSARY

admonish To express warning or disapproval.

ascribe To assign as a source.

berate To insult harshly and repeatedly.

carpetbagger A politician who doesn't originally reside where he or she is running for office.

caucus A meeting of members of a political party, called to select candidates.

commencement A ceremony at which diplomas or degrees are handed out to students who have completed a course of study.

congressman (or representative) An official, elected by people in his or her state, who represents those people in the U.S. House of Representatives.

constituents The people a politician represents in his or her elected post.

culpable Guilty; worthy of blame.

daunting Discouraging, inspiring fear.

dysentery An intestinal infection that causes chronic diarrhea and bleeding.

527 group A tax-exempt group that is independent but whose main purpose is to influence the nomination or election of a candidate.

garner To gather something, usually information or positive comments.

Geneva Convention One of a series of treaties that govern international laws on humanitarian concerns. Article Three of the Geneva Convention addresses the treatment of prisoners of war.

G.O.P. Acronym for the Grand Old Party, the Republican Party.

hazing The process by which a group of people initiate new members into their group by requesting physically demeaning or dangerous behavior and/or emotionally humiliating tasks.

insolent Insultingly contemptuous; overly bold or proud.

jibe Insult or ridicule.

lineage Group tracing descent from a common ancestor.

lobbyist A person or group of people organized to influence politicians or a political body on a specific issue.

midshipman (midshipwoman) Person in training for a naval commission, especially one enrolled in a naval academy.

plebe First-year student at a military or naval academy.

primary The election or elections held before the general election to determine which candidates will represent their party in the main election.

remorse Deep and painful regret for wrongdoing.

self-effacing Tending to stay in the background; humble.

senator An official elected to represent a state in the U.S. Senate.

soft money Money donated to political parties that is not regulated by federal election laws.

stint Period of time spent at a regular activity.

vehemently With vigor and passion.

viable Capable of functioning; workable.

FOR MORE INFORMATION

Republican National Committee
310 First Street SE
Washington, DC 20003
(202) 863-8500
Web site: http://www.GOP.com

Straight Talk America
211 North Union Street, Suite 200
Alexandria, VA 22314
Web site: http://www.straighttalkamerica.com

United States Naval Academy
121 Blake Road
Annapolis, MD 21402-5000
(410) 293-1000
Web site: http://www.usna.edu///homepage.php

United States Senate
Office of Senator (Name)
Washington, DC 20510
Web site: http://www.senate.gov

C
A
R
E
E
R

P
R
O
F
I
L
E
S

Web Sites

Due to the changing nature of Internet links, the Rosen Publishing Group, Inc., has developed an online list of Web sites related to the subject of this book. This site is updated regularly. Please use this link to access the list:

http://www.rosenlinks.com/cp/jomc

FOR FURTHER READING

Alexander, Paul. *John McCain, Man of the People*. New York, NY: Wiley Press, 2002.

Day, Kathleen. *S&L Hell: The People and the Politics Behind the $1 Trillion Savings and Loan Scandal*. New York, NY: Norton, 1993.

Downs, Frederick. *The Killing Zone: My Life in the Vietnam War*. New York, NY: Norton, 1993.

Ehrenreich, Barabara, and John Gray, et al. *Abu Ghraib: The Politics of Torture*. Berkeley, CA: North Atlantic Books, 2005.

Haddock, Dorris, and Dennis Burke. *Granny D: Walking Across America in My Ninetieth Year*. New York, NY: Villard, 2001.

Johnson, Brad W., and Greg P. Harper. *Becoming a Leader the Annapolis Way*. New York, NY: McGraw Hill, 2004.

McCain, John, and Mark Salter. *Character Is Destiny*. New York, NY: Random House, 2005.

McCain, John, and Mark Salter. *Faith of My Fathers*. New York, NY: Random House, 1999.

McCain, John, and Mark Salter. *Why Courage Matters: The Way to a Braver Life*. New York, NY: Random House, 2004.

Timberg, Robert. *John McCain: An American Odyssey.* New York, NY: Touchstone, 1999.

Whitney, David C. *The American Presidents: Biographies of the Chief Executives from George Washington to George W. Bush.* Pleasantville, NY: Reader's Digest, 2001.

BIBLIOGRAPHY

Duffy, Michael, and Nancy Gibbs. "Fathers, Sons, and Ghosts." *Time*. February 28, 2000. Retrieved September 2006 (http://www.cnn.com/ALLPOLITICS/time/2000/02/21/fathers.html).

Feinberg, Barbara Silberdick. *John McCain Serving His Country*. Brookfield, CT: Millbrook Press, 2000.

Frankel, Glenn. "The McCain Makeover." WashingtonPost.com. August 27, 2006. Retrieved October 2006 (http://www.washingtonpost.com/wp-dyn/content/article/ 2006/08/23/AR2006082301586_pf.html).

Gibbs, Nancy, and John F. Dickerson. "The Power and the Story." *Time*, in partnership with CNN. December 13, 1999. Retrieved October 2006 (http://www.time.com/time/magazine/article/0,9171,992801,00.html).

Gross, Terry. "Shaping Characters and Destinies: John McCain." National Public Radio. December 6, 2005. Retrieved September 2006 (http://www.npr.org/templates/story/story.php?storyId=5039481).

Harkavy, Jerry. "McCain: New School Students Need a Lesson in Courtesy." Associated Press. May 21, 2006. Retrieved October 2006 (http://www.boston.com/news/local/maine/articles/2006/05/21/mccain_new_school_students_need_lesson_in_courtesy/).

Krugman, Paul. "The Right's Man." NYTimes.com. March 13, 2006. Retrieved October 2006 (http://select.nytimes.com/2006/03/13/opinion/13krugman.html?hp).

Larry King Live (transcript). November 3, 2005. Retrieved October 2006 (http://transcripts.cnn.com/TRANSCRIPTS/0511/03/lkl.01.html).

Lawrence, Jill. "Once-Foe McCain Makes Friend of Bush Dynasty." USAtoday.com. April 10, 2006. Retrieved October 2006 (http://www.usatoday.com/news/washington/2006-04-09-mccain _x.htm).

McCain, John. "McCain Calls for Common Sense Conservatism at GOPAC Dinner." November 16, 2006. Retrieved December 21, 2006 (http://www.mccain.senate.gov/press_office/view_article.cfm?ID=770).

McCain, John, and Mark Salter. *Faith of My Fathers*. New York: NY: Random House, 1999.

Muller, Bill. "John McCain, America's Maverick Senator." *Arizona Republic*. October 1999.

Retrieved September 2006 (http://www.
azcentral.com/specials/special39/).

Sammon, Bill. "Meet the Next President—McCain
the Maverick." Examiner.com. September 15,
2006. Retrieved October 2006 (http://www.
examiner.com/a287263~Meet_the_Next_
President__McCain_the_Maverick.html).

Tapper, Jake. "McCain Files Federal Complaint."
Salon.com. March 6, 2006. Retrieved October
2006 (http://archive.salon.com/politics2000/
feature/2000/03/06/fec/).

Tapper, Jake. "McCain Wins Big." Salon.com.
February 2, 2000. Retrieved October 2006
(http://archive.salon.com/politics2000/
feature/2000/02/02/mccain/index.html).

Timberg, Robert. *John McCain: An American Odyssey.*
New York, NY: Touchstone, 1999.

INDEX

About the Author

Kira Wizner is a writer living in New York City. She is a former middle school English and humanities teacher and staff developer in the New York City public school system. She has worked helping students understand political campaigns in middle school classrooms for ten years. Having a cousin who died in a prisoner-of-war camp in Korea, she has a particular interest in the Geneva Convention and its efficacy today. Her husband is a public school teacher and writer. She is the proud mother of two girls.

Photo Credits

Cover © Rusty Russell/Getty Images; pp. 5, 78–79 © Paul J. Richards/AFP/Getty Images; pp. 9, 13, 25, 66, 69 © Terry Ashe/Time Life Pictures/Getty Images; p. 11 © Corbis; p. 21 © John Phillips/Time Life Pictures/Getty Images; pp. 24, 30 © Corbis Sygma; p. 27 www.news.navy.mil; pp. 32–33 © Bettmann/Corbis; pp. 35, 37 © AFP/Getty Images; pp. 40, 43, 47, 51 © AP/Wide World Photos; p. 49 © Getty Images; p. 54 © Corbis Sygma; p. 58 © Time Magazine/Time & Life Pictures/Getty Images; p. 65 © Cynthia Johnson/Time Life Pictures/Getty Images; p. 72 © Luke Frazza/AFP/Getty Images; p. 74 © John Mottern/AFP/Getty Images; p. 81 © Henny Ray Abrams/AFP/Getty Images; p. 83 (top) © Michael Smith/Newsmakers/Getty Images; p. 83 (bottom) © Alex Wong/Getty Images; p. 85 © Tim Sloan/AFP/Getty Images; pp. 90–91 © Scott Nelson/Getty Images; p. 94 www.exploremccain.com.

Designer: Tahara Anderson; **Editor:** Chris Roberts;
Photo Researcher: Amy Feinberg

STORAGE